THIS *book*
BELONGS TO

_____

DEDICATION

This TV Show Tracker book is dedicated to all the dedicated and organized people out there who want to keep track of all the tv shows they watch.

Your are my inspiration for producing books and I'm honored to be a part of keeping all your tv notes and shows all in one place.

This TV Show Tracker journal notebook will help you record your details, notes and schedules about your television shows.

Thoughtfully put together with these sections to record: Must Watch List, Name Of Show, Seasons, Episodes, The Ending, Notes & Thoughts & Rating.

HOW TO USE THIS BOOK

The purpose of this book is to keep all of your lists and notes all in one place. It will help keep you organized.

This TV Show Tracker Journal will allow you to accurately document all of your favorite tv shows schedule, and details. It's a great way to chart your course through the land of TV.

Here are examples of the prompts for you to fill in and write about yourself in this book:

Must Watch List - With tick boxes.
Name Of Show - Which show you are watching.
Seasons - How many seasons & which season you are watching.
Episodes - Which episode you are watching.
The Ending - How it ends & if you were happy with the ending.
Notes & Thoughts - Any other important detailed you'd like to record such as favorite actors or actresses or your review of the show.
Rating - A place for you to rate the show 1-5 stars.

TV shows
MUST WATCH!

- ◯
- ◯
- ◯
- ◯
- ◯
- ◯
- ◯
- ◯
- ◯
- ◯
- ◯
- ◯
- ◯

TV shows
MUST WATCH!

- ◯
- ◯
- ◯
- ◯
- ◯
- ◯
- ◯
- ◯
- ◯
- ◯
- ◯
- ◯
- ◯

TV show

NAME:
SEASONS:
EPISODES:

SEASON:

THE ENDING

-Thoughts-

Rating:

TV show

NAME:
SEASONS:
EPISODES:

SEASON:

THE ENDING

-Thoughts-

Rating:

TV show

NAME:
SEASONS:
EPISODES:

SEASON:

THE ENDING

-Thoughts-

Rating:

TV show

NAME:
SEASONS:
EPISODES:

SEASON:

THE ENDING

-Thoughts-

Rating:

TV show

NAME:
SEASONS:
EPISODES:

SEASON:

THE ENDING

-Thoughts-

Rating:

TV show

NAME:
SEASONS:
EPISODES:
SEASON:

THE ENDING

-Thoughts-

Rating:

TV show

NAME:
SEASONS:
EPISODES:

SEASON:

THE ENDING

-Thoughts-

Rating:

TV show

NAME:
SEASONS:
EPISODES:

SEASON:

THE ENDING

-Thoughts-

Rating:

TV *show*

NAME:
SEASONS:
EPISODES:

SEASON:

THE ENDING

-Thoughts-

Rating:

TV

NAME:
SEASONS:
EPISODES:

SEASON:

THE ENDING

-Thoughts-

Rating:

TV show

NAME:
SEASONS:
EPISODES:

SEASON:

THE ENDING

-Thoughts-

Rating:

TV show

NAME:
SEASONS:
EPISODES:

SEASON:

THE ENDING

-Thoughts-

Rating:

TV show

NAME:
SEASONS:
EPISODES:

SEASON:

THE ENDING

-Thoughts-

Rating:

TV show

NAME:
SEASONS:
EPISODES:

SEASON:

THE ENDING

-Thoughts-

Rating:

TV show

NAME:
SEASONS:
EPISODES:

SEASON:

THE ENDING

-Thoughts-

Rating:

TV show

NAME:
SEASONS:
EPISODES:

SEASON:

THE ENDING

-Thoughts-

Rating:

TV show

NAME:
SEASONS:
EPISODES:

SEASON:

THE ENDING

-Thoughts-

Rating:

TV show

NAME:
SEASONS:
EPISODES:

SEASON:

THE ENDING

-Thoughts-

Rating:

TV Show

NAME:
SEASONS:
EPISODES:

SEASON:

THE ENDING

-Thoughts-

Rating:

TV show

NAME:
SEASONS:
EPISODES:

SEASON:

THE ENDING

-Thoughts-

Rating:

TV show

NAME:
SEASONS:
EPISODES:

SEASON:

THE ENDING

-Thoughts-

Rating:

TV *show*

NAME:
SEASONS:
EPISODES:

SEASON:

THE ENDING

-Thoughts-

Rating:

TV show

NAME:
SEASONS:
EPISODES:

SEASON:

THE ENDING

-Thoughts-

Rating:

TV show

NAME:
SEASONS:
EPISODES:

SEASON:

THE ENDING

-Thoughts-

Rating:

TV show

NAME:
SEASONS:
EPISODES:

SEASON:

THE ENDING

-Thoughts-

Rating:

TV show

NAME:
SEASONS:
EPISODES:

SEASON:

THE ENDING

-Thoughts-

Rating:

TV show

NAME:
SEASONS:
EPISODES:

SEASON:

THE ENDING

-Thoughts-

Rating:

TV show

NAME:
SEASONS:
EPISODES:

SEASON:

THE ENDING

-Thoughts-

Rating:

TV show

NAME:
SEASONS:
EPISODES:

SEASON:

THE ENDING

-Thoughts-

Rating:

TV show

NAME:
SEASONS:
EPISODES:

SEASON:

THE ENDING

-Thoughts-

Rating:

TV show

NAME:
SEASONS:
EPISODES:

SEASON:

THE ENDING

-Thoughts-

Rating:

TV show

NAME:
SEASONS:
EPISODES:

SEASON:

THE ENDING

-Thoughts-

Rating:

TV show

NAME:
SEASONS:
EPISODES:

SEASON:

THE ENDING

-Thoughts-

Rating:

TV show

NAME:
SEASONS:
EPISODES:

SEASON:

THE ENDING

-Thoughts-

Rating:

TV

NAME:
SEASONS:
EPISODES:

SEASON:

THE ENDING

-Thoughts-

Rating:

TV show

NAME:
SEASONS:
EPISODES:

SEASON:

THE ENDING

-Thoughts-

Rating:

TV show

NAME:
SEASONS:
EPISODES:

SEASON:

THE ENDING

-Thoughts-

Rating:

TV show

NAME:
SEASONS:
EPISODES:

SEASON:

THE ENDING

-Thoughts-

Rating:

TV

NAME:
SEASONS:
EPISODES:

SEASON:

THE ENDING

-Thoughts-

Rating:

TV show

NAME:
SEASONS:
EPISODES:

SEASON:

THE ENDING

-Thoughts-

Rating:

TV show

NAME:
SEASONS:
EPISODES:

SEASON:

THE ENDING

-Thoughts-

Rating:

TV show

NAME:
SEASONS:
EPISODES:

SEASON:

THE ENDING

-Thoughts-

Rating:

TV show

NAME:
SEASONS:
EPISODES:

SEASON:

THE ENDING

-Thoughts-

Rating:

TV show

NAME:
SEASONS:
EPISODES:

SEASON:

THE ENDING

-Thoughts-

Rating:

TV show

NAME:
SEASONS:
EPISODES:

SEASON:

THE ENDING

-Thoughts-

Rating:

TV show

NAME:
SEASONS:
EPISODES:

SEASON:

THE ENDING

-Thoughts-

Rating:

TV show

NAME:
SEASONS:
EPISODES:

SEASON:

THE ENDING

-Thoughts-

Rating:

TV show

NAME:
SEASONS:
EPISODES:

SEASON:

THE ENDING

-Thoughts-

Rating:

TV show

NAME:
SEASONS:
EPISODES:

SEASON:

THE ENDING

-Thoughts-

Rating:

TV show

NAME:
SEASONS:
EPISODES:

SEASON:

THE ENDING

-Thoughts-

Rating:

TV show

NAME:
SEASONS:
EPISODES:

SEASON:

THE ENDING

-Thoughts-

Rating:

TV show

NAME:
SEASONS:
EPISODES:

SEASON:

THE ENDING

-Thoughts-

Rating:

TV show

NAME:
SEASONS:
EPISODES:

SEASON:

THE ENDING

-Thoughts-

Rating:

TV Show

NAME:
SEASONS:
EPISODES:

SEASON:

THE ENDING

-Thoughts-

Rating:

TV show

NAME:
SEASONS:
EPISODES:

SEASON:

THE ENDING

-Thoughts-

Rating:

TV show

NAME:
SEASONS:
EPISODES:

SEASON:

THE ENDING

-Thoughts-

Rating:

TV show

NAME:
SEASONS:
EPISODES:

SEASON:

THE ENDING

-Thoughts-

Rating:

TV show

NAME:
SEASONS:
EPISODES:

SEASON:

THE ENDING

-Thoughts-

Rating:

TV show

NAME:
SEASONS:
EPISODES:

SEASON:

THE ENDING

-Thoughts-

Rating:

TV show

NAME:
SEASONS:
EPISODES:

SEASON:

THE ENDING

-Thoughts-

Rating:

TV show

NAME:
SEASONS:
EPISODES:

SEASON:

THE ENDING

-Thoughts-

Rating:

TV show

NAME:
SEASONS:
EPISODES:

SEASON:

THE ENDING

-Thoughts-

Rating:

TV show

NAME:
SEASONS:
EPISODES:

SEASON:

THE ENDING

-Thoughts-

Rating:

TV show

NAME:
SEASONS:
EPISODES:

SEASON:

THE ENDING

-Thoughts-

Rating:

TV show

NAME:
SEASONS:
EPISODES:

SEASON:

THE ENDING

-Thoughts-

Rating:

TV show

NAME:
SEASONS:
EPISODES:

SEASON:

THE ENDING

-Thoughts-

Rating:

TV show

NAME:
SEASONS:
EPISODES:

SEASON:

THE ENDING

-Thoughts-

Rating:

TV show

NAME:
SEASONS:
EPISODES:

SEASON:

THE ENDING

-Thoughts-

Rating:

TV show

NAME:
SEASONS:
EPISODES:

SEASON:

THE ENDING

-Thoughts-

Rating:

TV show

NAME:
SEASONS:
EPISODES:

SEASON:

THE ENDING

-Thoughts-

Rating:

TV *show*

NAME:
SEASONS:
EPISODES:

SEASON:

THE ENDING

-Thoughts-

Rating:

TV
show

NAME:
SEASONS:
EPISODES:

SEASON:

THE ENDING

-Thoughts-

Rating:

TV Show

NAME:
SEASONS:
EPISODES:

SEASON:

THE ENDING

-Thoughts-

Rating:

TV show

NAME:
SEASONS:
EPISODES:

SEASON:

THE ENDING

-Thoughts-

Rating:

TV show

NAME:
SEASONS:
EPISODES:

SEASON:

THE ENDING

-Thoughts-

Rating:

TV show

NAME:
SEASONS:
EPISODES:

SEASON:

THE ENDING

-Thoughts-

Rating:

TV show

NAME:
SEASONS:
EPISODES:

SEASON:

THE ENDING

-Thoughts-

Rating:

TV show

NAME:
SEASONS:
EPISODES:

SEASON:

THE ENDING

-Thoughts-

Rating:

TV *show*

NAME:
SEASONS:
EPISODES:

SEASON:

THE ENDING

-Thoughts-

Rating:

TV show

NAME:
SEASONS:
EPISODES:

SEASON:

THE ENDING

-Thoughts-

Rating:

TV show

NAME:
SEASONS:
EPISODES:

SEASON:

THE ENDING

-Thoughts-

Rating:

TV show

NAME:
SEASONS:
EPISODES:

SEASON:

THE ENDING

-Thoughts-

Rating:

TV show

NAME:
SEASONS:
EPISODES:

SEASON:

THE ENDING

-Thoughts-

Rating:

TV show

NAME:
SEASONS:
EPISODES:

SEASON:

THE ENDING

-Thoughts-

Rating:

TV *show*

NAME:
SEASONS:
EPISODES:

SEASON:

THE ENDING

-Thoughts-

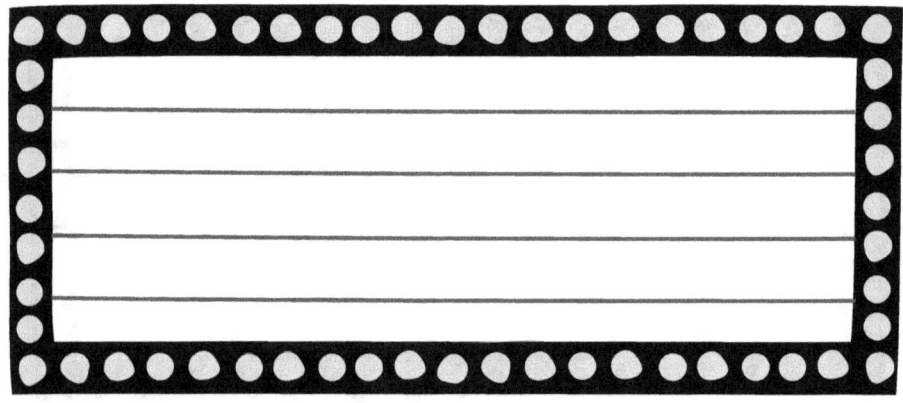

Rating:

TV show

NAME:
SEASONS:
EPISODES:

SEASON:

THE ENDING

-Thoughts-

Rating:

TV show

NAME:
SEASONS:
EPISODES:

SEASON:

THE ENDING

-Thoughts-

Rating:

TV show

NAME:
SEASONS:
EPISODES:

SEASON:

THE ENDING

-Thoughts-

Rating:

TV show

NAME:
SEASONS:
EPISODES:

SEASON:

THE ENDING

-Thoughts-

Rating:

TV show

NAME:
SEASONS:
EPISODES:

SEASON:

THE ENDING

-Thoughts-

Rating:

TV show

NAME:
SEASONS:
EPISODES:

SEASON:

THE ENDING

-Thoughts-

Rating:

TV Show

NAME:
SEASONS:
EPISODES:

SEASON:

THE ENDING

-Thoughts-

Rating:

TV show

NAME:
SEASONS:
EPISODES:

SEASON:

THE ENDING

-Thoughts-

Rating:

www.ingramcontent.com/pod-product-compliance
Lightning Source LLC
Chambersburg PA
CBHW071409080526
44587CB00017B/3220